THE GARDEN OWNER'S SURVIVAL GUIDE

By Martin Baxendale

Published by Silent But Deadly
Publications, 21 Bisley Road,
Stroud, Glos., GL5 1HF

Printed in England by
Stoate & Bishop Printers Ltd,
Shaftesbury Industrial Centre,
Cheltenham, Glos. GL51 9NH

ISBN: 978-0-9562398-1-5

INTRODUCTION

Of course gardening can be very enjoyable, even relaxing (so I'm told) but other times it can feel like a never-ending uphill battle that you stand absolutely no chance at all of ever winning.

I've been gardening for more years than I care to remember, and there are still plenty of days when it feels like I'm being slowly driven round the bend by the constant watering, weeding, cutting-back and tidying-up, and by the endless struggle against the slugs, snails, greenfly and other pests, not to mention the weather (please don't mention the bloody weather!) And I know I'm not the only one, so I do hope readers will find the following pages, based on my own experiences, helpful.

Now if you'll excuse me, I'm off to spend some time shouting at the slugs and snails from my back door.

My therapist thinks it may prove therapeutic and help stop the red mists and the garden rage that always seems to end up in carnage with headless garden gnomes everywhere and neighbours peering worriedly over fences. Mrs Baxendale, my dear wife, says if the police are called just once more, she's taking away my snail mallet for a whole week.

YOU SLIMY LITTLE BASTARDS!
I'M GOING TO GET YOU!
SLUG
PELLETS
20 kilos
My favourite snail-bashing mallet.

ESSENTIAL GARDENING EQUIPMENT

Of course all gardeners need certain basic tools and equipment - spade, trowel, rake, secateurs, watering can, snail mallet, etc. The following are rather less obvious but equally important gardening essentials which you should never be without:

1) Super-Soaker water-blaster gun for discouraging neighbourhood cats from using your garden as a public toilet.
2) Extra-large pack of disposable rubber gloves for picking cat-pooh out of soil (actually, make that two packs...no, three...oh, just get lots and lots).
3) Industrial quantities of slug pellets (they're cheaper by the lorry load).
4) A gardening diary in which you can record every little annoying failure, frustration and defeat of the gardening year, as well as your utter hatred and loathing of all things slimy, sluggy and snaily, and how you're going to kill them all, then kill them again (my therapist says this is very therapeutic).
5) A garden shed in which to hide when it all gets a bit too much and you feel like having a nice nervous breakdown.

Step **away** from the bed of newly planted seedlings! Okay, Tiddles, you asked for it!
MIAOW!!
SWOOSH!

Sob! Bloody slugs and snails! I **hate** them! I **hate** them!
POUR TEA IN HERE
KEEP OUT!

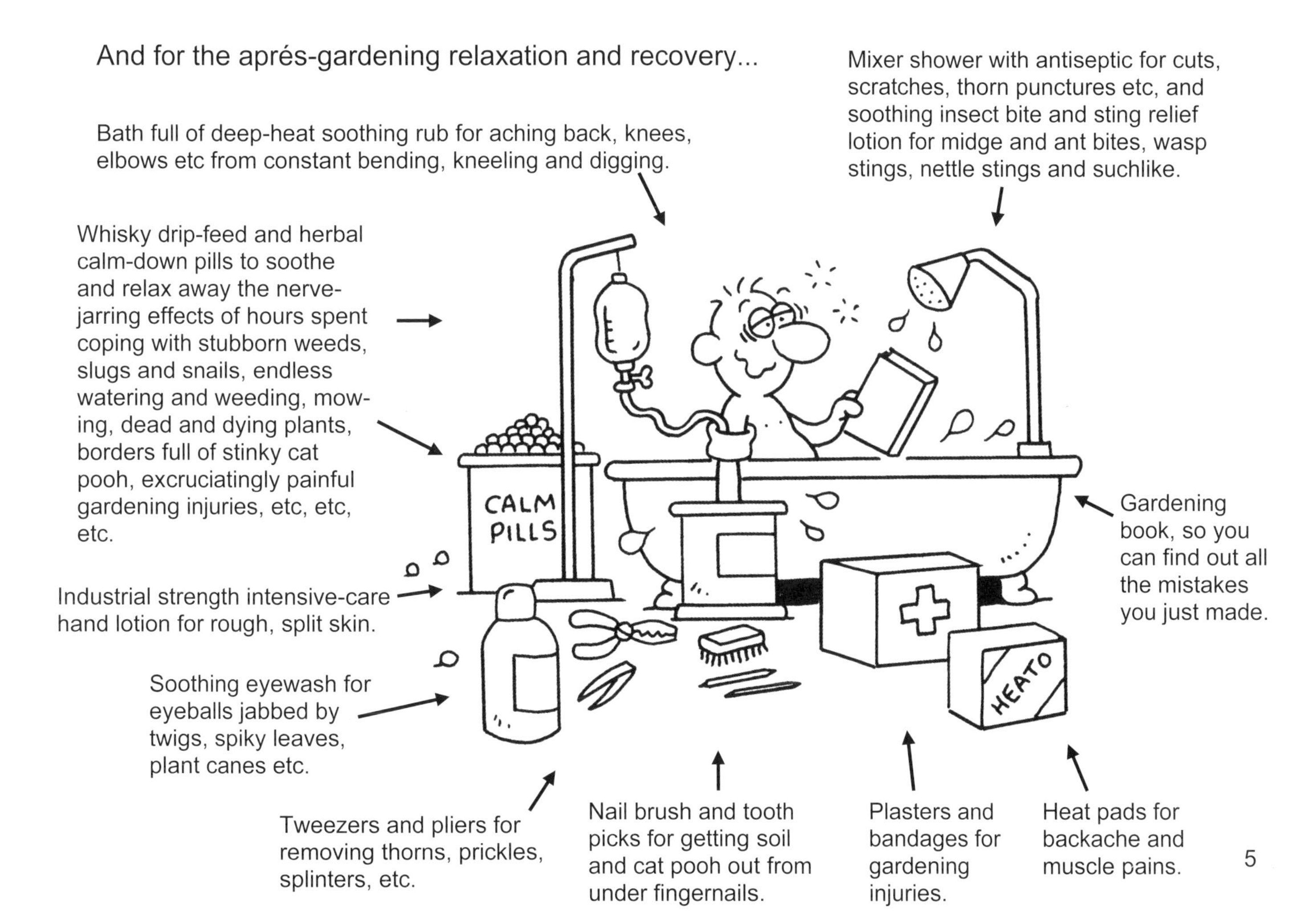
And for the aprés-gardening relaxation and recovery...
Bath full of deep-heat soothing rub for aching back, knees, elbows etc from constant bending, kneeling and digging.
Mixer shower with antiseptic for cuts, scratches, thorn punctures etc, and soothing insect bite and sting relief lotion for midge and ant bites, wasp stings, nettle stings and suchlike.
Whisky drip-feed and herbal calm-down pills to soothe and relax away the nerve-jarring effects of hours spent coping with stubborn weeds, slugs and snails, endless watering and weeding, mowing, dead and dying plants, borders full of stinky cat pooh, excruciatingly painful gardening injuries, etc, etc, etc.
CALM PILLS
Gardening book, so you can find out all the mistakes you just made.
Industrial strength intensive-care hand lotion for rough, split skin.
HEATO
Soothing eyewash for eyeballs jabbed by twigs, spiky leaves, plant canes etc.
Tweezers and pliers for removing thorns, prickles, splinters, etc.
Nail brush and tooth picks for getting soil and cat pooh out from under fingernails.
Plasters and bandages for gardening injuries.
Heat pads for backache and muscle pains.

RECOMMENDED SAFETY EQUIPMENT

Perhaps not everyone will feel the need for all the safety equipment suggested here, but I've suffered so many gardening-related mishaps, injuries and traumas over the years that these days I don't take any risks at all.

Insect-repellent spray to keep midges, wasps, ants etc at bay.

Goggles to protect eyes from twigs when pruning, from spiky leaves, garden canes and sticks, and from flying bits of snail shell when using my snail mallet.

Riot shield for protection against thorny, spiky, scratchy plants, stinging nettles and flying bits of snail shell when using my snail mallet.

Riot helmet (okay, so I wear this mostly to stop my hair getting messed up by twigs and branches, and because it looks cool).

Thorn-proof gauntlets.

Earplugs to stop earwigs crawling inside my ears (oh yes they do!)

Thorn-proof trousers and thorn-proof underpants (you can't be too careful).

Strap-on kneeling pads.

Thornproof jacket (body armour is optional).

Steel-toecap wellies to protect against accidental foot-stabbing incidents with garden forks, of which I've had more than a few.

Aching backs and knees from bending and kneeling in the garden are a common complaint amongst gardeners, especially as they get on a bit. Of course you can treat the symptoms (and you will have to) but preventative action will also help.

An easy-to-make device that reduces back-ache and knee problems from constant bending and kneeling. You should be able to knock it up in your garden shed.

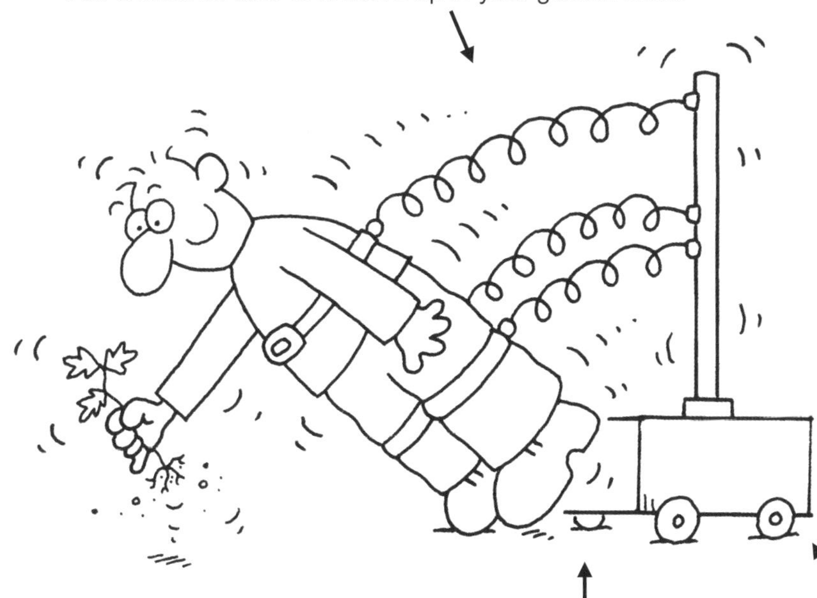

Springs enable you to lean right down to the ground and stand back up again without having to bend your back or kneel.

Wheeled base weighted down with rocks.

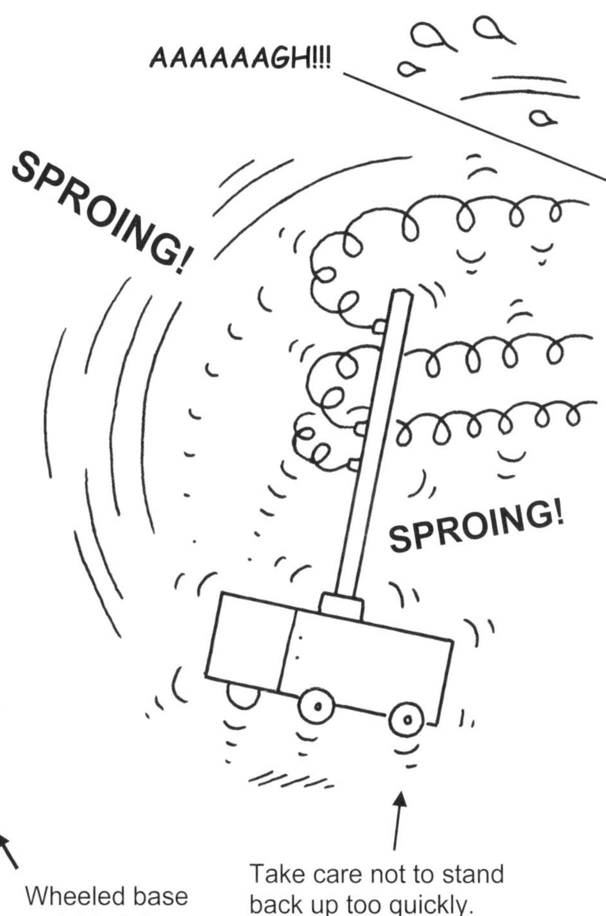
AAAAAAGH!!!
SPROING!
SPROING!

Take care not to stand back up <u>too quickly</u>.

Alternatively, there's the equally easy-to-make weeding harness with helium-filled balloons. Especially good for working on the middles of very wide beds and borders (and, with extra helium in the balloons, also handy for cutting back tall shrubs, trees and hedges without having to mess about with ladders).

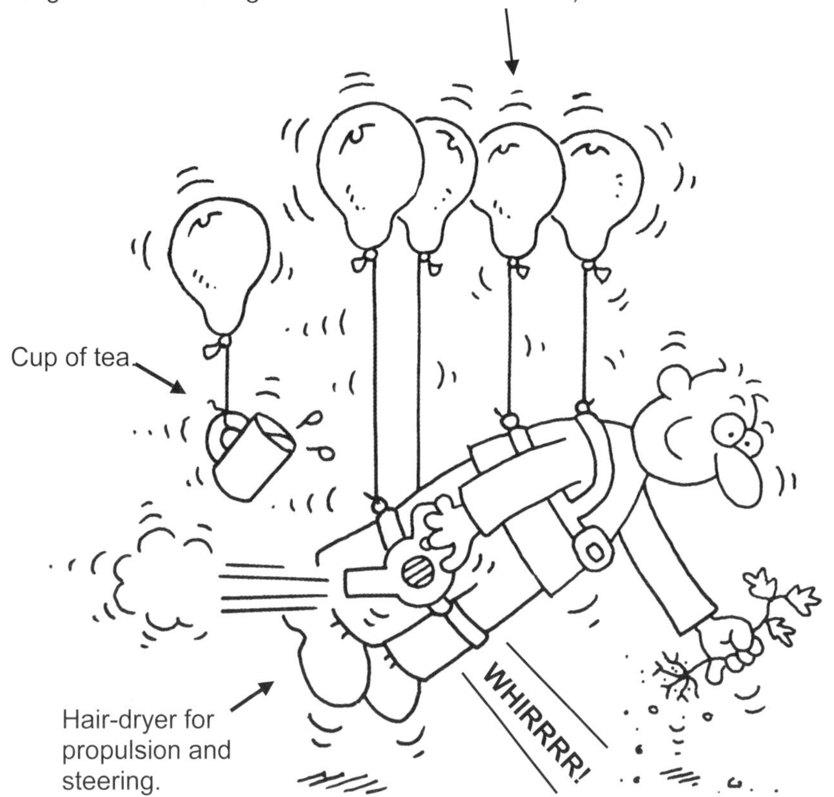
Cup of tea
WHIRRRRR!
Hair-dryer for propulsion and steering.

HELP!!
GUST!
GUST!

But not really suitable for use on windy days (or around spiky plants and shrubs).

GARDEN PLANNING

Gardening books always go on about the importance of planning your garden and your plantings, and of course you can if you want. It's just that I gave up all of that years ago when it became clear that whatever I might plan, the garden always had other ideas - usually to turn itself into an impenetrable jungle the moment my back was turned.

And this is my carefully planned **white** border...with just a few blue flowers...and some red flowers...and one or two pink...and yellow...and purple....

Also, like most gardeners, I can't resist the urge to keep squeezing in one more plant here, there and everywhere, until any vague planting scheme or plan I might have started with is just a distant memory.

"Don't try to squeeze a quart into a pint pot" the gardening books also advise. Like they'll ever stop gardeners constantly nibbling away at their lawns, making their beds and borders ever bigger and wider in the hope of fitting in just a few more plants. Mrs Baxendale thinks I may have taken things just a bit too far, but it's really all a matter of opinion, don't you think?

In her opinion, apparently you've gone too far if you can't actually see the lawn any more.

I'm telling you, the lawn's in here **somewhere**. Just keep looking.

However, I am finally, after a great many mistakes too awful to even think about, let alone admit to, starting to grudgingly accept that one very important part of garden planning is choosing plants to suit the size of the garden and the situation.

Ooh, that's a bargain! Let's get **two**!
Giant Redwood seedlings £1-99p (Note: eventual height 300ft)
I **told** you putting that fast-growing creeper on the wall of the house would cause problems!

It's not always easy, though!
It says "Needs a planting site that gets morning sun, afternoon shade and evening semi-shade. Doesn't like sunsets and will die if exposed to moonlight".
It's also important, when planning your garden planting schemes, to hide any eyesores. And this, she informs me, is Mrs Baxendale's own special planting idea to hide me from her view when we're both in the garden.
There's no point glaring at me. I can't see you.

SLUGS AND SNAILS

I actually have nightmares about slugs and snails when the weather's wet, although the therapy is helping and I no longer have to sleep with my snail mallet under the pillow (much to the relief of Mrs Baxendale, who claimed that being kept awake by my snoring and occasionally getting whacked with a mallet in the middle of the night was getting her down a bit).

Slugs and snails must be the most hated of garden pests and the ones that drive gardeners crazy more than any other, and no wonder; on damp summer evenings you can actually hear them eating their way through the garden like a giant free buffet.

Mrs Baxendale says that's ridiculous, that she can't hear a thing. But I'm telling you, some nights it's so loud I have to wear earplugs.

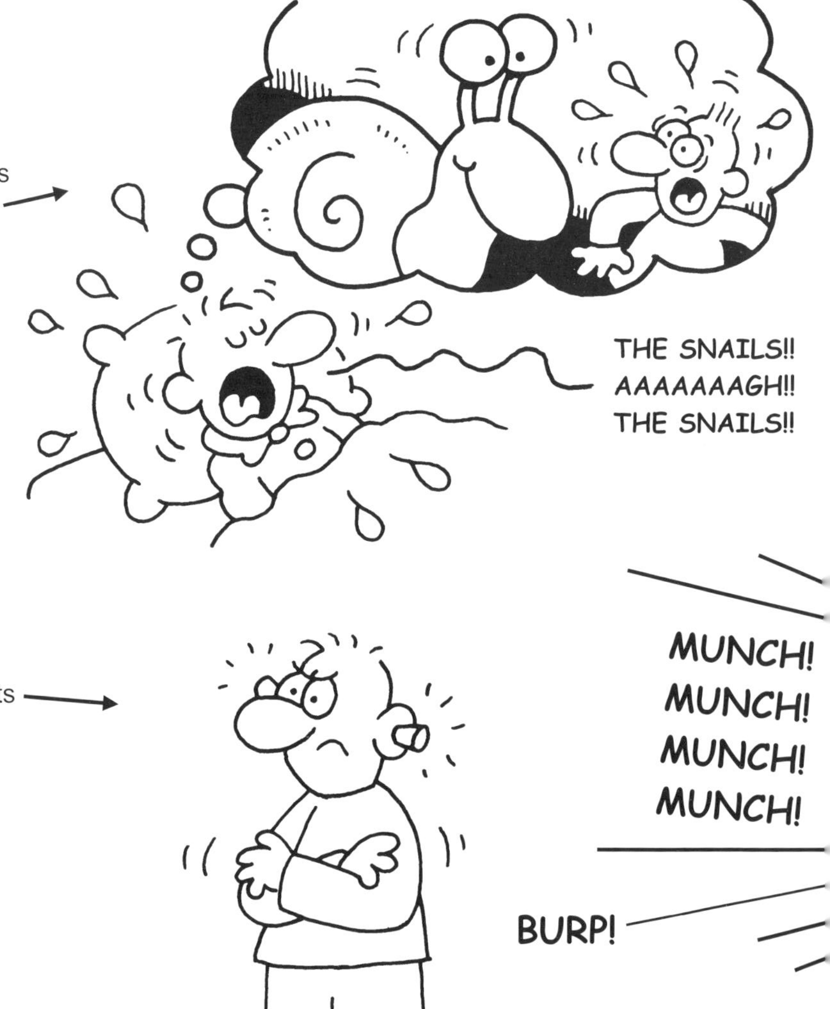
THE SNAILS!!
AAAAAAAGH!!
THE SNAILS!!
MUNCH!
MUNCH!
MUNCH!
MUNCH!
BURP!

The first line of defence for most gardeners is slug pellets, and I have to admit I use them myself - in moderation of course, in fact quite sparingly because Mrs Baxendale says it's not good for the wildlife to use too many.

Some people swear by beer traps - jam jars sunk into the soil with beer in them. The slugs and snails are supposed to get drunk on the beer, fall in and drown.

Never works for me. Not sure why, but I hardly ever find any slugs or snails in my jars. Plus, when I run out of beer in the evening, it's just too tempting to nip out and grab a jarful from the garden (yes, it's flat and occasionally a bit slimy, but better than no beer at all).

Delivery for Mr Baxendale...lorry load of loose slug pellets. Where d'you want 'em?
Oh, er....just tip them straight onto the garden. I'll rake them level later.

Eugh!! It's his crappy **home-brew** again! I'm not drinking that stuff!
SNIFF!
They've got **Carlsberg Special Brew** next door!
Hic!
SPLOSH!

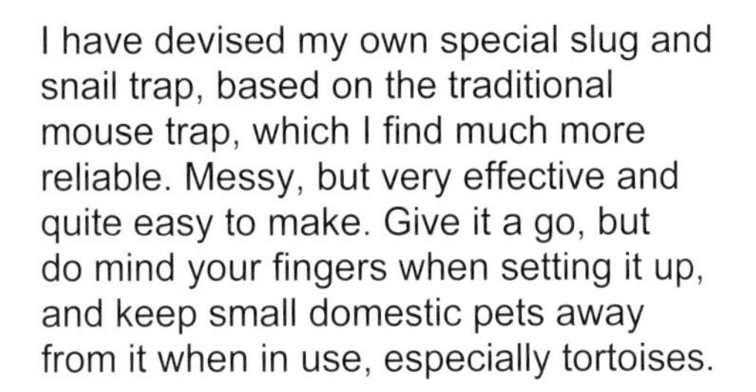

I have devised my own special slug and snail trap, based on the traditional mouse trap, which I find much more reliable. Messy, but very effective and quite easy to make. Give it a go, but do mind your fingers when setting it up, and keep small domestic pets away from it when in use, especially tortoises.

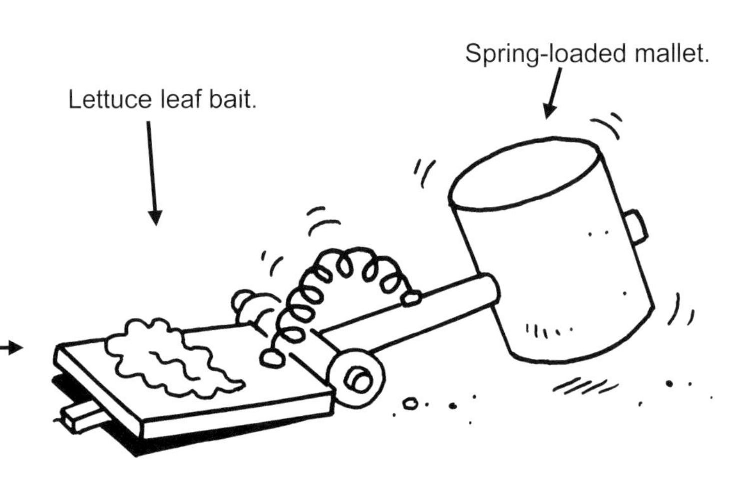
Spring-loaded mallet.
Lettuce leaf bait.
Weight of snail or slug on bait platform triggers mallet.

BOOM!

MY NEW BEDDING PLANTS!!

I'm also working on a prototype for mini anti-snail and anti-slug landmines but current anti-terrorism legislation forbids me showing you how to make these (anyway, I'm still having some problems getting the size of the explosive charge just right).

Of course you can always just pick up snails and lob them into next door's garden, especially if you don't get on with your neighbours. Problem is, they often just crawl back to their home turf.

I favour using a catapult to get them a few gardens up the road, so they're less likely to return. But do watch out for green-houses and hard-to-spot sunbathers lying on lawns.

OUCH !!!
SMASH!

GREENFLY

You have to be constantly on your guard for these little buggers. One minute there are none on a plant, the next there's millions of them. God knows where they come from! I suspect they're being sent through hyperspace from another dimension as "presents" to humankind from an alien race for whom greenfly are a rare delicacy. Well enough already! If the aliens are listening, WE DON'T WANT ANY MORE, THANK YOU! OH, AND WOULD YOU LIKE SOME SLUGS AND SNAILS?

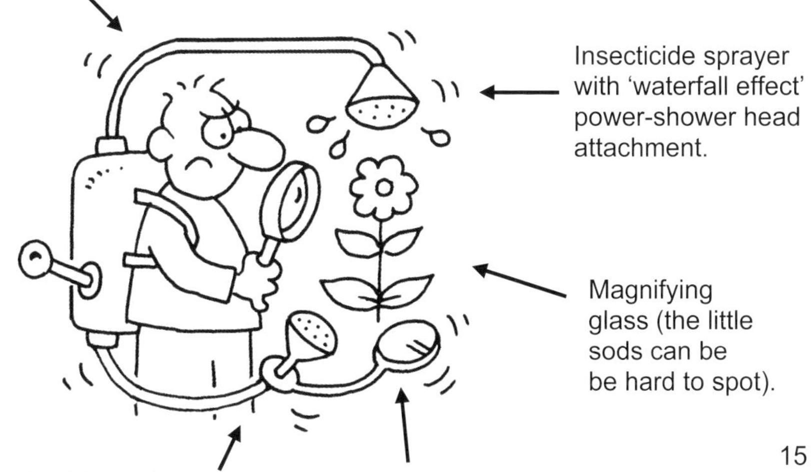
I can recommend my own highly effective patented anti-greenfly kit.
Insecticide sprayer with 'waterfall effect' power-shower head attachment.
Magnifying glass (the little sods can be be hard to spot).
For spraying undersides of leaves.
Mirror for checking undersides of leaves.

OTHER GARDEN PESTS

CATS:

Neighbours' cats coming into the garden and digging and pooing can be a real pain in the bum. Of course you may not consider your own cats to be quite so much of a problem (probably because they'll tend to go into other gardens to make a mess of things). But they can still be a nuisance if they decide to dig and poo on their own territory.

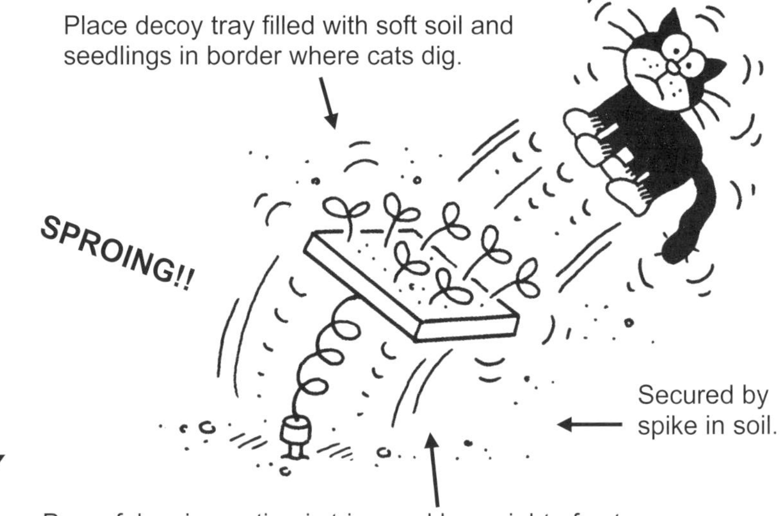
Place decoy tray filled with soft soil and seedlings in border where cats dig.
SPROING!!
Secured by spike in soil.
Powerful spring-action is triggered by weight of cat.

Please feel free to copy the design for my cat ejector device, which I've used in the garden for many years with great success. Use a larger or smaller spring to adjust the power to suit whether you want to train your own cat not to dig and poo in your borders, or to eject neighbours' cats back into nearby gardens (watch out for overhead power lines).

BONK!
See? I **told** you Tiddles can fly!

See also anti-cat water blaster, page 4.

NUISANCE NEIGHBOURS:

What're **you** doing? **I'm** feeding my **leylandii hedge**. It should grow **60 feet** tall if I don't prune it! I'm going to light a **huge bonfire** next.

These can be incredibly annoying and really spoil your enjoyment of your garden, whether inconsiderate, nosey or just downright obnoxious.

Introducing the Baxendale neighbour-snubbing device. I find it invaluable. With some basic tools, you could easily construct something similar.

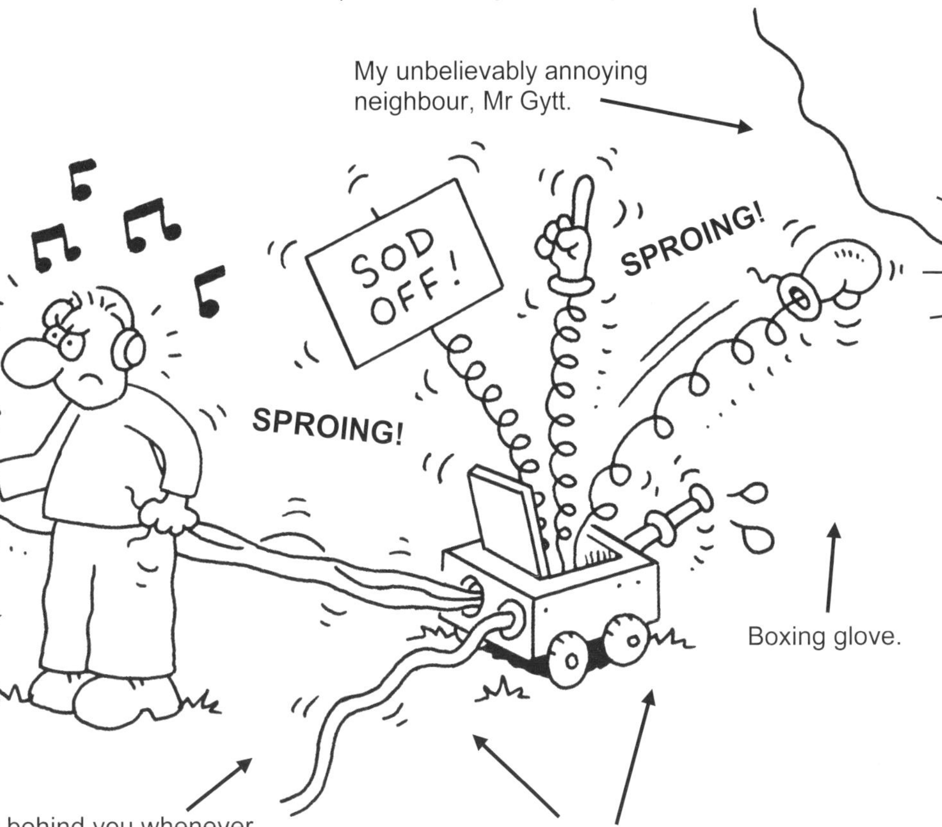
My unbelievably annoying neighbour, Mr Gytt.
SOD OFF!
SPROING!
SPROING!
Boxing glove.

Headphones to block out the nuisance neighbour's loud, annoying voice.

Strings operate spring release mechanisms and hosepipe on/off valve switch.

Pull along behind you whenever annoying neighbour is around.

Hosepipe.

In the event of habitual smoke nuisance from annoying neighbours - bonfires and/or stinky barbecues constantly filling your garden with acrid smoke - try this to get your own back. It works for me.

How do you want your **tyre burger**, dear? Well done?
WHIRRRR!
COUGH! COUGH!
Fan to blow smoke towards neighbours.

<u>CHILDREN</u>:

<u>Mrs</u> Baxendale and I disagree over whether children are pests in the garden. Let's just say it's best if kids can have their own play area or children's garden area, to avoid conflicts between their needs and those of the keen gardener.

THUD!
GOAL!!
SPLAT!

I would recommend a version of my cat ejector device (see page 16) to keep small children off beds and borders (whether your own kids or neighbourhood kids nipping over the fence to get their ball back or nick your apples) but → I'd probably get in trouble with Mrs Baxendale and the National Society for the Prevention of Cruelty to Annoying Children.

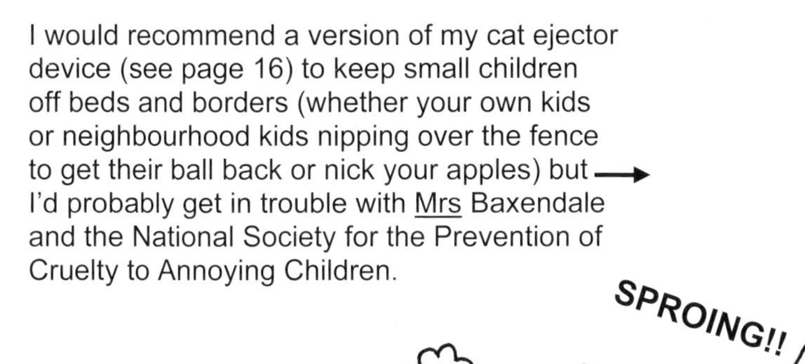
FLING!
SPROING!!

Mrs Baxendale and I also tend to disagree over what exactly constitutes an acceptable children's play area in the garden for our kids.

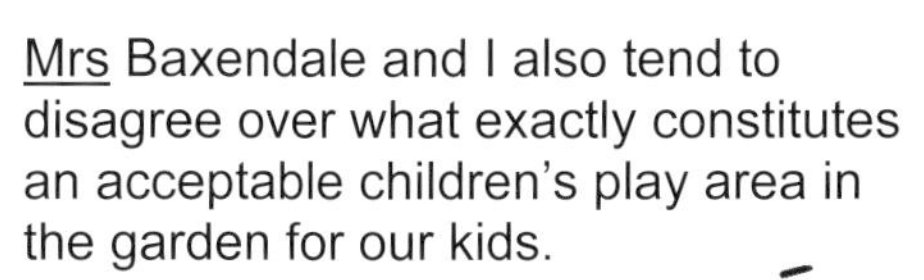

That's not a kids' play area.
It's a bloody **rabbit run**!

BOSSY 'HEAD GARDENERS':

When two people own a garden, a pecking-order will often develop with with one assuming the role of bossy 'Head Gardener' (often with a t-shirt emblazoned 'Head Gardener' to prove it) and the other basically doing what they're told.

In our garden, Mrs Baxendale has taken it upon herself to assume the bossy 'Head Gardener' role. If you possibly can, it's much better to nab this job for yourself. I really can't emphasise that too much. →

You missed a weed!
Sorry, Boss! Getting it now, Boss!
CRACK!

PLANT THIEVES:

The theft of valuable plants and shrubs from gardens, especially in ornamental pots and tubs, is becoming increasingly common. After the fourth clipped bay tree went walkies from outside our front door, I came up with this anti-theft plan to scare the poo out of thieves and then flatten them. Yes, I could just have just chained the tub to the wall, but that would have looked unsightly and wouldn't have been nearly as much fun. ←

CLICK!
This explosive device will detonate in three seconds...one...two...

← Wire attached to bag of cement precariously balanced on house roof or up a tree.

← Tape recorder disguised as a landmine.

MYSTERY GARDEN PESTS:

Finally, there are those mystery animal pests that get into the garden while you're asleep and dig (and sometimes poo) everywhere. It can drive you crazy trying to figure out exactly what creature is ploughing its way through your flower beds and veg patch night after night. Fox? Badger? Something else? Whatever it is, trust me, you'll go equally crazy trying to fence it out (and failing).

Could be a fox or badger, but I still say those look like **elephant** footprints. Exactly how far **are** we from the zoo?

How the hell did **you** get in?!

GARDEN BOUNDARIES:

Which brings me to my ongoing search for the perfect garden boundary, one which will keep out all garden pests and nuisances.

I really don't care if Mrs Baxendale and my therapist have looked at my preliminary plans and laughed themselves silly over them; I'm talking 15ft walls with electrified barbed-wire fencing on top, piranha-filled moat, watch towers with automatic anti-cat water-cannon, anti-snail and slug high-powered lasers, anti-annoying neighbour stun guns, etc, etc...

WEEDING AND WATERING

Weeding and watering are endless, thankless tasks that drive gardeners potty. After one summer-long drought, complete with the inevitable hosepipe ban, I couldn't look at a watering can without bursting into tears. And years of futile battling with deep-rooting bindweed have left me with a permanent nervous twitch in one eye and an irrational fear of deep holes.

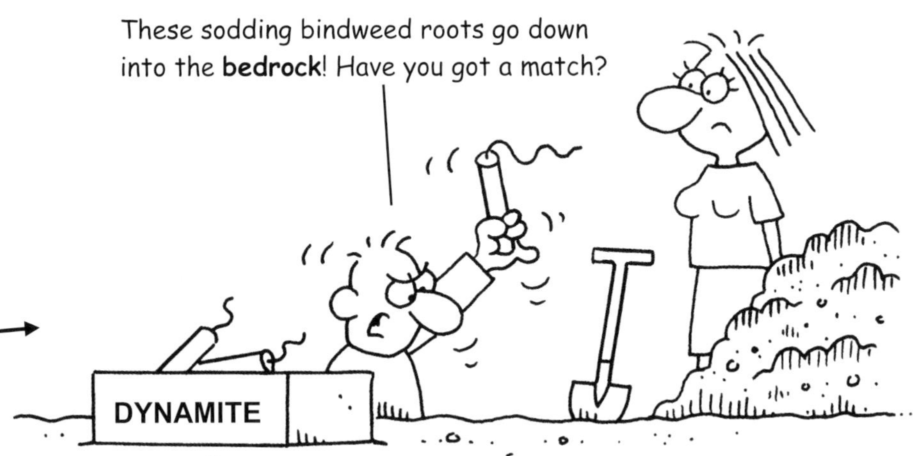
These sodding bindweed roots go down into the **bedrock**! Have you got a match?
DYNAMITE

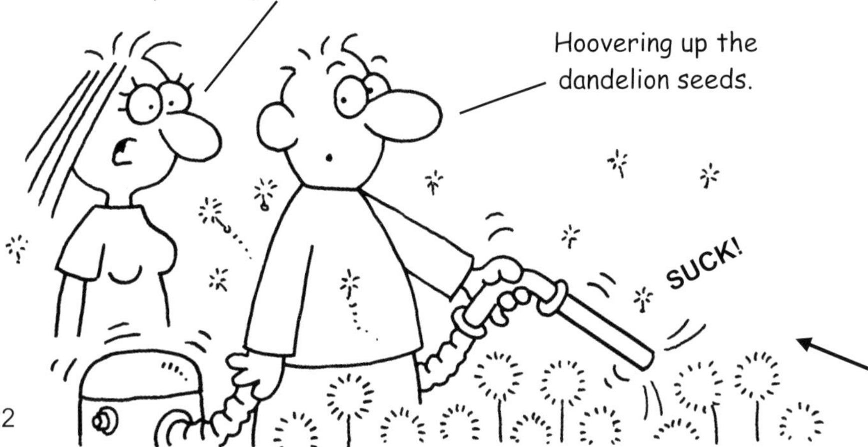
What are you doing with the vacuum cleaner?
Hoovering up the dandelion seeds.
SUCK!

The books always tell you that the golden rule of weed control is to never let them seed; or as my granddad used to say, "A year's seedin' means a life-time's weedin', an' that'll just drive a man right round the bend, like your uncle Albert who took to wearin' a marrow for a hat and thought pixies were stealin' 'is parsnips. Now eat up yer manure, it's good for ye".

Good advice (except for the manure bit of course) but somehow I never seem to catch my weeds in time.

I mostly hand-weed. Partly because my therapist says tearing the bastards out by the roots is much more therapeutic than spraying them. But mostly because it's so easy to get spray drifting onto plants and shrubs if your beds and borders are packed full like mine (and most other gardeners I know).

I will use spot-treatments on stubborn deep-rooting weeds in positions where it's awkward to dig them out, but I save larger-scale spraying for only the very biggest problems.

Our neighbour's enormous leylandii hedge that blocks out all our sunlight appears to be **dying**.
Yes. I do hope I didn't get a little **spray drift** on it when I was weed-killing this dandelion.
200 LTR.

A deep mulch will help to keep down the weeds, and also reduce the need for watering, but take care not to make it too deep. I have to admit I did get a bit carried away one year when the endless weeding got to me a bit.

Twenty lorry-loads of bark chippings.

Right, let's see those bloody dandelion seedlings come up through **this**!

Miaow!

I've devised the perfect answer to the problem of constant daily watering during dry summer weather. The idea came to me when a neighbour's shed caught fire and the fire brigade arrived to put it out (yes, it might have been my incredibly annoying neighbour Mr Gytt's shed, and yes I might have been aiming roman candles and rockets at it on bonfire night, but the police couldn't prove anything).

This is especially useful for getting around hosepipe bans in drought summers.

1) Make dummy garden shed out of old cardboard boxes and set it alight. **2)** Call fire brigade.

3) Sit back and watch as firemen arrive with their huge hoses. Tell them the garden is tinder-dry and all the plants and shrubs should also be hosed down in case sparks from the shed blow onto them and the fire spreads.

That's the **fourth** shed fire you've had this week, Mr Baxendale. Just exactly how many garden sheds do you **have**?

MOWING AND LAWN MAINTENANCE

Mowing the lawn is another never-ending chore, but I may have an answer for this too. It came to me just last week as I surveyed the slug-eaten plants in the borders next to the long grass of the lawn waiting to be cut yet again.

"Why don't slugs and snails eat bloody grass?!" I thought. Then, "A-hah! What if they did?" Of course this is all still in the experimental stages, and I can't guarantee it'll work, but it has to be worth a try, don't you think?

As an added refinement, I'm also developing the Snail-O-Mow ®™ Snail Harness which, combined with the Snail-O-Mow ®™ Essence Of Lettuce lawn treatment (see top right of page) should make me a fortune.

This works on the principle that if the snails are tethered to the lawn, then they'll bloody well have to eat the grass or starve. Of course you will have to catch and harness a lot of snails, but in most gardens it shouldn't be a problem finding enough.

Liquidise lettuce leaves (the grotty old ones from the outsides will do) and water or spray onto your lawn to attract the slugs and snails. Let me know if this works for you. If the results are encouraging, I'm planning on marketing a bottled essence of lettuce called Snail-O-Mow ®™ (too late, I've already patented it, so hands off, it's my idea!)

MUNCH!
Mmmm! This grass tastes just like **lettuce**! Why have I never tried it before?

Sucker attached to shell of snail, and fishing line tied to sucker.

?

Spring-loaded spool allows snail to gradually move outwards in its search for fresh grass to eat, until limit of fishing line is reached.

Bare patches on your lawn can be a real nuisance, constantly needing to be re-seeded, fertilised, watered and not walked on until re-established.

OR...do what I do - simply allow the grass on one side of the bald patch to grow very long and then comb (sorry, I mean rake) it over to hide the bare area. Don't know where I got the idea from, but it works a treat.

My dear wife's brother.

SUPPORTING FLOPPY PLANTS

I find the problem with using canes and sticks for supporting floppy plants is that the plants can quickly out-grow their supports and need taller replacements. Plus I keep jabbing my sodding eye out on them.

This is a much simpler answer. Not, however, suitable for very spiky-leaved plants.

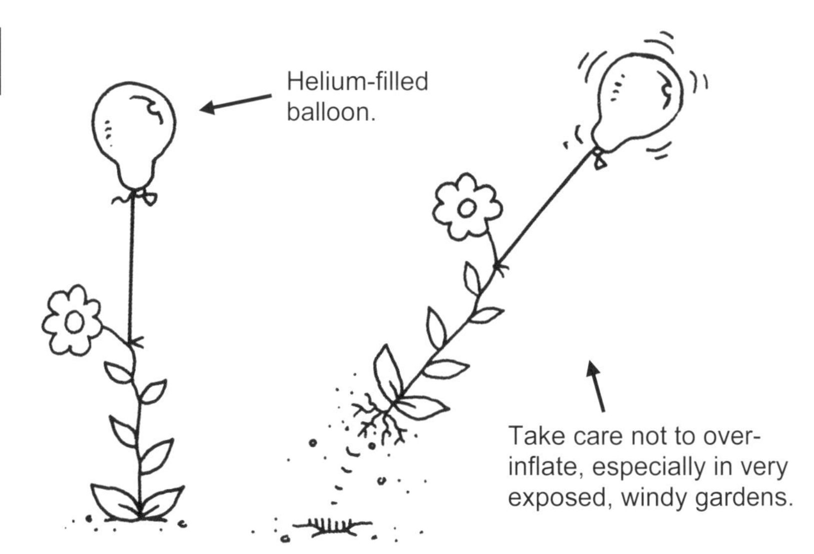
Helium-filled balloon.
Take care not to over-inflate, especially in very exposed, windy gardens.

PRUNING AND CUTTING BACK

Deciding how you're supposed to prune shrubs and trees can be a real puzzle, so here's a very simple guide based on how I usually do it:

1) Cut out any dead or diseased wood.
2) Thin out any very congested growth.
3) Prune to reduce size if necessary.
4) Go inside and check gardening book.
5) Discover you've cut off the wrong bits.
6) Glue the bits you shouldn't have cut off back on.
7) Look nonchalant.

Been pruning again?
GLUE

Heads we chop it back now. Tails we go inside and spend all day looking through gardening books trying to find out the 'right' time to prune it.

Deciding if it's the right time of year to prune a certain shrub or tree can also be difficult.

I tend to follow my granddad's wise advice passed on to me as a small boy helping in his garden: "Best time to do any job in't garden is when you 'ave the time to do it. Now stop askin' awkward questions and I'll let ye 'ave a puff on me pipe."

THE WEATHER

Gardening is of course a constant battle against the damn weather, which is always too wet or too dry, too cold or too hot, too snowy, too windy, too drizzly, etc, etc.

There's not much you can actually do about the weather, but never forget that as a gardener it is your sworn duty to always grumble about it, no matter what it's like.

And now the long-range weather report for gardeners. This week will be too wet, next week will be too dry, and the week after that will be **perfect** for gardening...only kidding, it will of course be too wet again.

WILT
Why won't it rain?! We don't need more **sunshine**! We want some bloody **rain**!!
Oh, **shut up!!**
WILT!

<u>Frost</u> is one thing you <u>can</u> do something about, protecting tender plants from cold snaps with horticultural fleece, bubble wrap etc. But in an emergency all kinds of everyday household materials - newspapers, old sheets etc - can be used instead (and will save you money).

Hey! Where's the **duvet** gone off our bed?!

Mum! I can't find my **hot water bottle**!

Mum! Why's Dad out in the snow in his pyjamas with your **hair dryer?**

WHIRRRR!

13

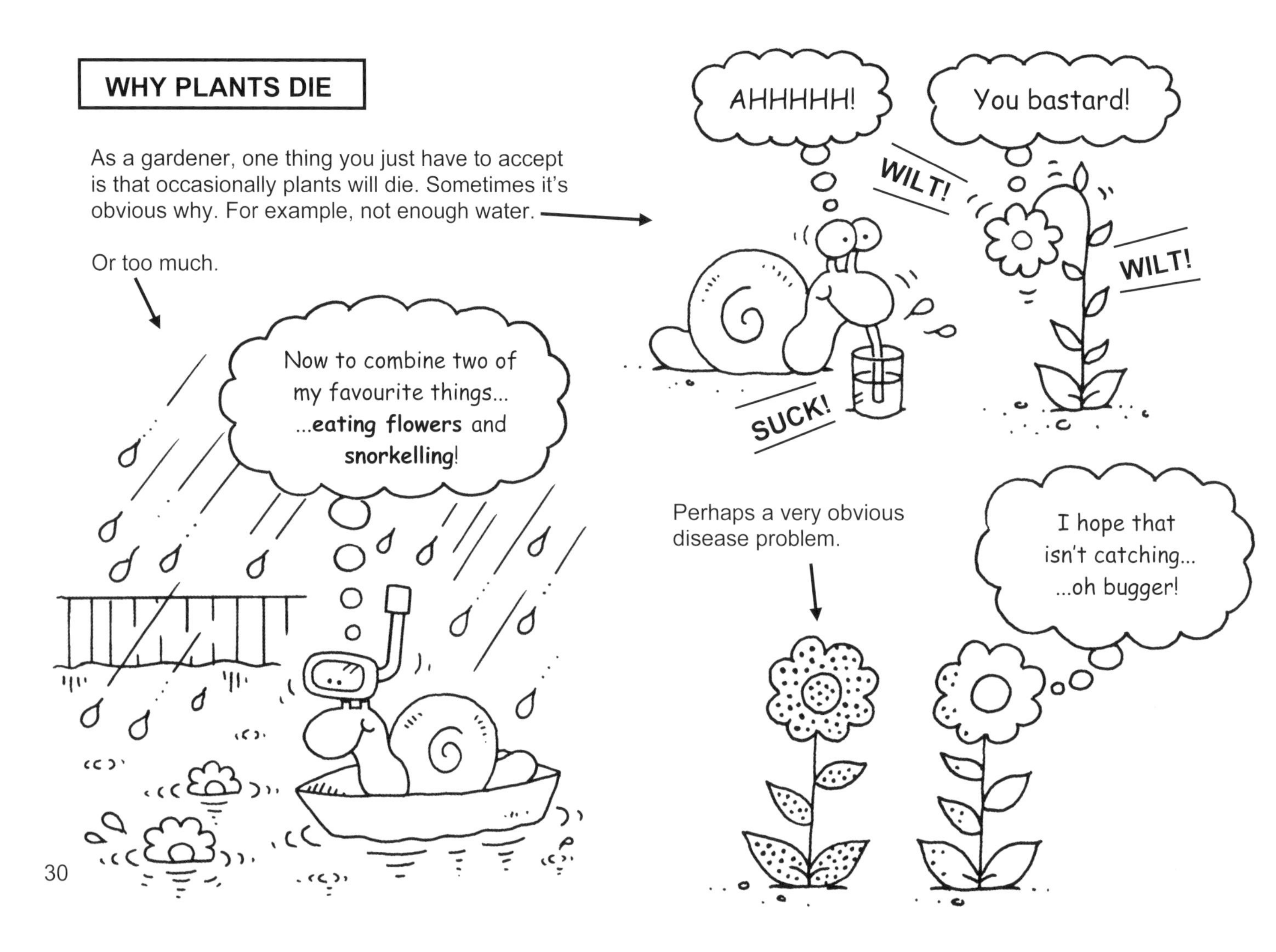
WHY PLANTS DIE
As a gardener, one thing you just have to accept is that occasionally plants will die. Sometimes it's obvious why. For example, not enough water.
AHHHHH!
You bastard!
WILT!
WILT!
SUCK!
Or too much.
Now to combine two of my favourite things... ...eating flowers and snorkelling!
Perhaps a very obvious disease problem.
I hope that isn't catching... ...oh bugger!

Or maybe because of an unusually cold winter.

But often plants will just up and die for no apparent reason - maybe just to annoy you, or because you looked at them a bit funny; who knows?

It's better not to obsess about it. Just move on, plant something else and enjoy that. Whatever you do, don't keep the old labels from dead plants as some kind of sad memento or record of what you used to grow.

Some gardeners do, and I did too until Mrs Baxendale pointed out that:

A) You couldn't move in the garden shed, garage and attic for boxes of 'dead' plant labels.

B) I had about a million times more labels for dead plants than I had live plants in the garden, and that collecting, looking through and cataloguing dead plant labels had in fact taken over from gardening as my main hobby.

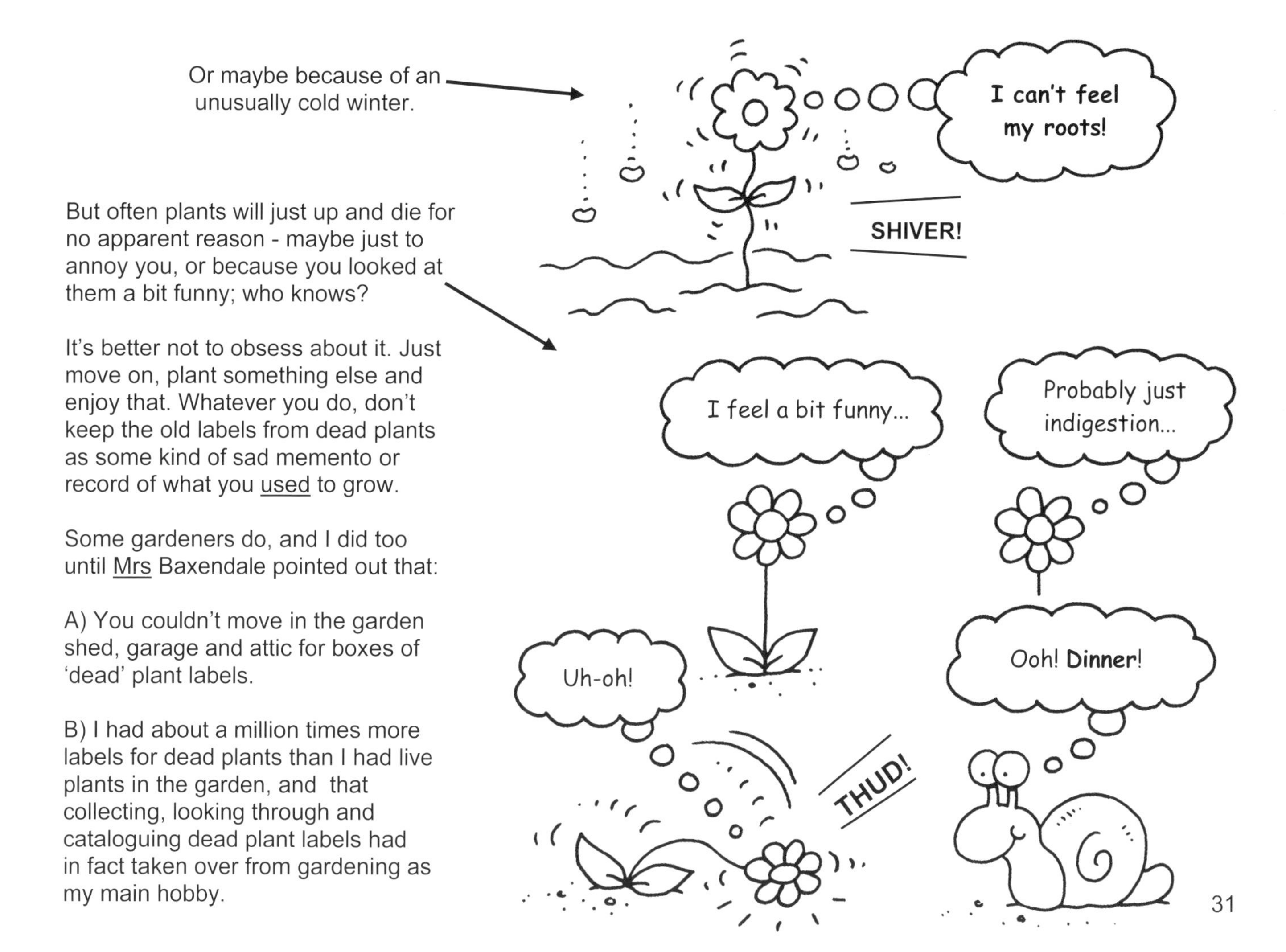

I can't feel my roots!
SHIVER!
I feel a bit funny...
Probably just indigestion...
Uh-oh!
THUD!
Ooh! **Dinner**!

OTHER BOOKS BY MARTIN BAXENDALE

'THE SNOWDROP GARDEN' - Martin's first novel is a wickedly funny and heart-warming tale of love, misunderstandings and a last-ditch attempt to save one of England's most beautiful woodland snowdrop gardens from the builders' bulldozers. A really great, laugh-out-loud read.

'WHEN WILL MY BABY BRAIN FALL OUT?' - Martin's first children's book. Seven-year-old Millie struggles with her maths homework but then she gets hold of the idea that things will be better when her 'baby brain' falls out, just like a baby tooth, and her cleverer big-girl brain grows in its place. Should Mum and Dad put her straight or play along? A very funny yet charming story that will have children laughing out loud.

And some of Martin's best-selling cartoon gift-books:

'Your New Baby, An Owner's Manual' (over 500,000 copies sold).
'How To Be A Baby, An Instruction Manual For Newborns'
'Your Marriage, An Owner's Manual'
'How To Be Married, An Instruction Manual For Newlyweds'
'Life After 40, A Survival Guide For Women'
'Life After 40, A Survival Guide For Men'
'Life After 50, A Survival Guide For Women'
'Life After 50, A Survival Guide For Men'
'How To Stay Awake During Sex (and other handy hints on coping with old age)'
'Martin Baxendale's Better Sex Guide'
'The Relationship Survival Guide'
'A Very Rude Book About Willies'
'The Cat Owner's Survival Guide'
'The Dog Owner's Survival Guide'
'Your Man, An Owner's Manual'
'Calm Down!! The Stress Survival Guide'
'Your Pregnancy, A Survival Guide'
'Women Are Wonderful, Men Are A Mess'

These and other books by Martin Baxendale can be ordered from www.amazon.co.uk (search for Martin Baxendale, or search by title, in 'books') and from other online bookstores or any High Street bookshop.